WHAT AM I FEELING?

John Gottman, Ph.D. and Talaris Research Institute
Photographs by Talaris Research Institute

Parenting Press, Inc.
Chicago

Library of Congress Cataloging-in-Publication Data

Gottman, John Mordechai.
  What am I feeling? / John Gottman ; photographs by Talaris Research Institute.
    p. cm.
  Includes bibliographical references.
  ISBN 1-884734-52-9
  1. Emotions in children. 2. Child rearing. I. Title.

  BF723.E6G68 2004
  s 649'.7—dc22

                        2004008655

Publisher
Parenting Press, Inc.
814 North Franklin Street, Chicago, Illinois 60610
www.parentingpress.com

In cooperation with
Talaris Research Institute
P.O. Box 45040, Seattle, WA 98175
www.talaris.org

Table of Contents

ACKNOWLEDGMENTS

What Am I Feeling? *is based on*
Dr. John Gottman's research found in his book
entitled **Raising an Emotionally**
Intelligent Child: The Heart of Parenting.
Dr. Gottman and Talaris Research Institute
created this smaller book as an
introduction to emotions and emotion
coaching for parents and caregivers of children.

ABOUT TALARIS

Located in Seattle, Washington, Talaris Research Institute
is a non-profit organization dedicated to creating
tools for parents that help them effectively raise their
children. As part of its mission, Talaris scours the world
of research for information with practical applications
for parents. The research is evaluated and translated
into meaningful, easy-to-understand tools for parents.

Social and emotional development in children helps
to create a solid foundation for lifelong learning.
This book about "emotion coaching" is based on John
Gottman's book, *Raising An Emotionally Intelligent
Child*. Though targeted for those who nurture children,
this information can also help adults when dealing
with their own emotions and the emotions of others.
For more detailed information about the "Four Parenting
Styles" or the "Five Steps of Emotion Coaching," visit
the "Spotlight" section on **www.talaris.org**.

Emotions . . . we all have them. Everything we do and everything we learn are shaped in some way by the way we feel. These feelings are a natural part of who we are.

Sometimes emotions can be unpredictable. We can be happy in one moment and sad or angry in the next. Some of us are uncomfortable with our emotions and try to avoid them while others try to be aware of them and understand them. How we deal with our emotions can make a big difference in the quality of our lives.

We all have strong attitudes and beliefs about our feelings that begin when we're children. The way we feel about our own emotions— how we value them and how we cope with them—helps to shape how we parent and nurture children.

Research has found that children raised by parents who value and guide emotions do better in many ways.

* *These children form stronger friendships.*

* *They do better in school.*

* *They handle their moods better, have fewer negative emotions, and bounce back from emotional events more quickly.*

* *They even get sick less often.*

This book begins by helping you identify your parenting and caregiving style. Then it explains the five important steps in "emotion coaching." It will help you learn how to be an emotion coach, so that you can guide and nurture healthy emotional growth in children.

Accepting, valuing, sharing, and guiding emotions are not always easy . . . but are well worth the effort.

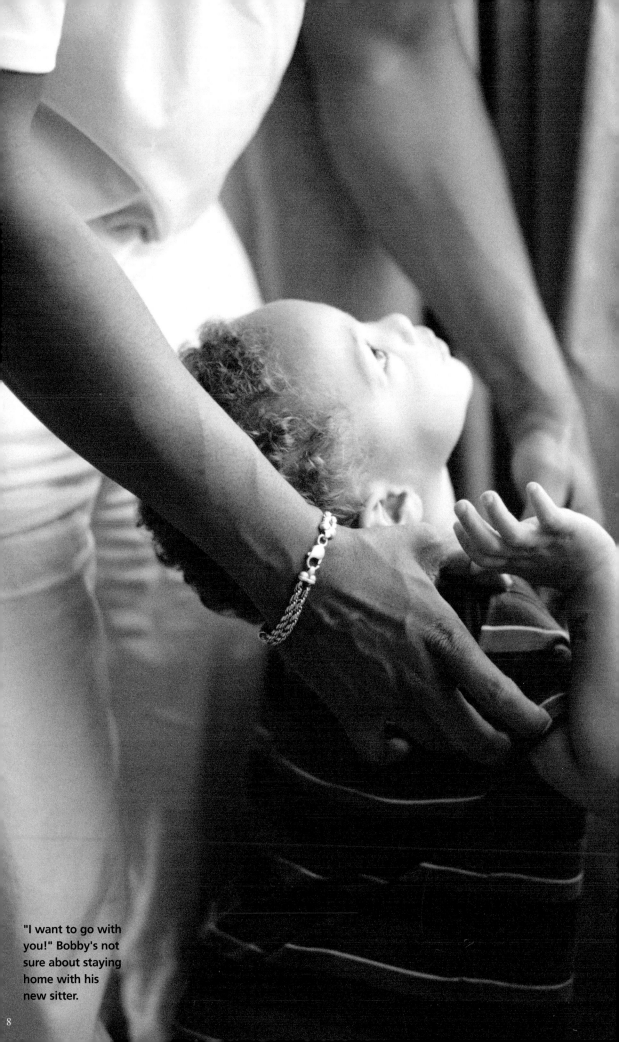

"I want to go with you!" Bobby's not sure about staying home with his new sitter.

IDENTIFYING YOUR PARENTING STYLE

What are your feelings about emotions? How do you handle the emotions of a child? Most of the time, adults respond to children's feelings in ways that match their own attitudes about emotions. In his research on families and emotions, Dr. John Gottman has identified four parenting styles. Most parents and caregivers tend to use one style more often than others. Keep in mind that these styles describe what parents and caregivers do most of the time, and that adults might use other styles during the course of a day or a week.

"I hurt my finger. Is Mom upset at me?" What is Brianne feeling?

Four Parenting Styles

The Dismissing Style

The Disapproving Style

The Laissez-Faire Style

The Emotion Coaching Style

"Where is my happy girl?"

The Dismissing Style

Ignoring "bad" emotions

A PARENT SAYS:

"You don't need to be sad. It's not that bad. Put a smile on your face. There's no reason to be unhappy."

A CHILD FEELS:

A child often feels ignored or disregarded when she has strong feelings. She learns to believe that emotions such as sadness and anger are "bad" and need to be fixed quickly. She doesn't learn how to handle her emotions, and has trouble with her feelings when she is upset.

There is no such thing as a "bad" emotion.
It's how we handle our emotions that matters.

Mom says "Don't worry, Eric, be happy!" Maybe Mom should listen to how Eric feels.

"Just get over it"

Some parents, caregivers, and teachers believe the best way to deal with children's emotions is to tell them to "just get over it." They tend to dismiss children's feelings because they don't think they're important or they don't know what else to do.

For instance, when a child says, "It makes me sad that I can't go to Grandma's," a dismissive adult might respond by saying, "Don't be sad, you'll see her in a couple of weeks. Let's go to the park and play."

These adults often feel uncomfortable if children are sad or angry. They believe negative emotions are harmful or unnecessary, and should be avoided. As a result, they might ignore the emotions, try to "fix" children's moods, or try to distract them from their feelings.

All of these reactions, although well meaning, fall short because in dismissing a child's feelings we:

* Risk diminishing or dismissing the child

* Suggest to the child that emotions aren't to be trusted

* Suggest experiencing sadness isn't important or shouldn't happen

* Create a pattern of dismissing emotions that the child learns and imitates

* Discourage the child from coming to you when he or she feels sad or angry

If this pattern of dismissing emotions sounds familiar, there are ways to change to a style that treats emotions differently. This style is emotion coaching. When you value and guide a child's emotions, many benefits follow—including the opportunity to grow much closer in your relationship.

"Quit pouting, you're the big brother!"

The Disapproving Style

"Bad" emotions are punished

A PARENT SAYS:

"Stop feeling that way. You have no reason to be sad, and
nobody wants a whiner around. If you keep that up, you'll
be in trouble."

A CHILD FEELS:

A child feels that something is wrong with him if he gets
upset or sad. He is criticized or punished for showing emotions
such as sadness or anger even when he does not misbehave.
His parents call these "bad" emotions. So, he doesn't
learn how to handle his strong feelings, and he struggles
with friendships.

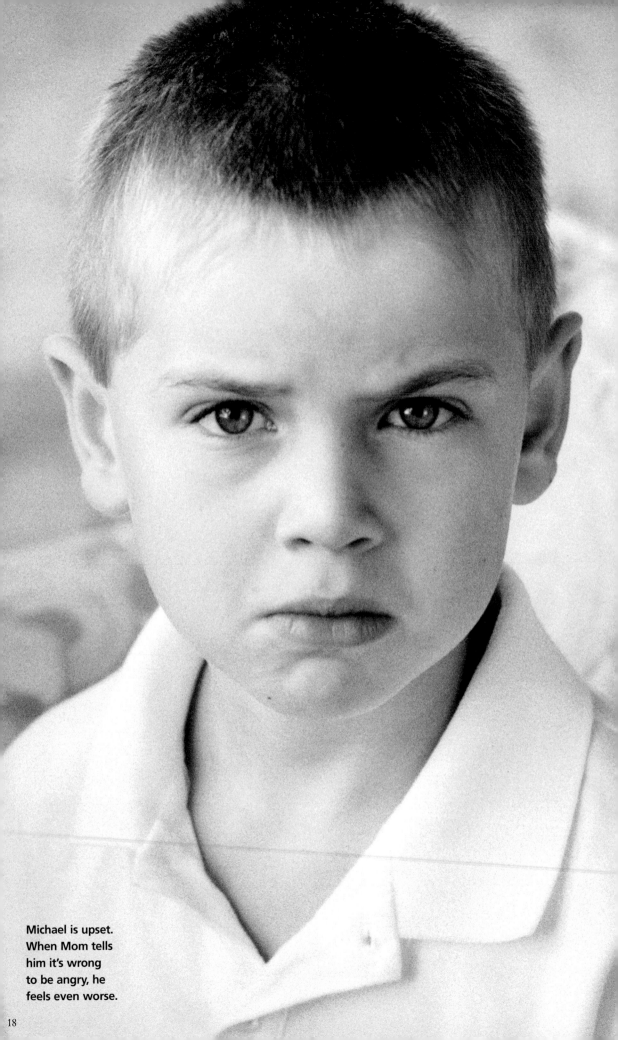

Michael is upset.
When Mom tells
him it's wrong
to be angry, he
feels even worse.

"You shouldn't feel that way"

Keesha is angry and about to cry. Her mom, who thinks Keesha just wants attention, disapproves of her daughter's anger and wants her to change her feelings. "Don't be a brat, Keesha." Keesha starts to cry. "Stop it right now. I said stop it!" More crying. "That's it, Keesha. If I hear any more crying, you'll be in trouble!" More crying, of course.

Now, not only is Keesha angry about something, but she is also in trouble for feeling that way. And she's about to be punished for the way she feels—as if she's misbehaved.

Keesha's mom disapproves of her daughter's negative emotions such as anger, fear, or sadness. Disapproving parents, caregivers, and teachers view these emotions as unacceptable and controllable, so instead of trying to understand children's emotions, they discipline or punish them for the way they feel.

The problem with this approach is that emotions cannot simply be switched on or off at will. Trying to make children turn them off can be harmful. Research shows children raised by disapproving parents:

* Have more difficulty trusting their own judgment

* Can grow up feeling something is wrong with them

* Are more likely to suffer from a lack of self-esteem

* Have trouble regulating their emotions and solving their problems

* Have more difficulty concentrating, learning, and getting along with peers than other children

The disapproving style does little to help children handle their emotions. Emotion coaching is the best way to teach children about their feelings and how to handle their emotions in positive ways.

*"I know you're excited,
but watch out for the baby."*

The Laissez-Faire Style

Emotions without guidance

A PARENT SAYS:

"That's it, just let the feelings out. Do what you need to do. It doesn't bother me. Whatever you feel like doing is okay."

A CHILD FEELS:

A child feels comfortable in expressing her feelings and knows that it is acceptable to show emotions whether she is happy, angry, or sad. But there are no limits on her behavior and there is little guidance on how to deal with emotions. She learns that her emotions are okay, but she doesn't learn how to handle them in appropriate ways.

Tommy is happy and is having a ball. When is it time to stop clowning around and clean up?

"Anything goes"

The French expression "laissez-faire" means "to leave something alone" or "to let it be." For some parents, caregivers, and teachers, this describes an attitude of total acceptance and non-interference with children's emotions. They want children to know that expressing emotions is a positive thing, and that no matter what their behavior is they will be loved.

This approach is good in many ways, but it doesn't do enough to nurture healthy emotional development. Encouraging children to experience their emotions is part of the puzzle, but they also need help understanding them. Part of nurturing emotional development includes setting limits on behavior. Children need to learn their feelings are okay, but not all behaviors are acceptable. Children need to be guided as they learn how to cope with their emotions. This is where the "laissez-faire" approach falls short.

Without this guidance, children don't learn how to handle their emotions and as a result they:

✳ Often lack the ability to calm down when angry, sad, or upset

✳ Find it more difficult to concentrate or learn new skills

✳ Find it more difficult to pick up on social cues, and, therefore, may find it harder to make and keep friends

Learning how to understand and manage emotions is important for everyone. Adults can help children by learning and practicing the five key steps of emotion coaching.

"I know you're upset.
So what would make you feel better?"

THE EMOTION COACHING STYLE

Empathy and guidance

A PARENT SAYS:

"Tell me how you feel. I've felt that way, too. And you can't hit somebody when you're angry. Let's think together about other things you can do when you feel this way."

A CHILD FEELS:

A child feels valued and comforted when all of her emotions are accepted. At the same time, she learns that there are limits on her behavior when she has strong feelings. She receives empathy when upset or angry and guidance in learning to deal with her emotions. She feels comfortable in expressing her emotions and she learns to trust her feelings and solve problems.

Carrie's big brother
has been teasing her.
Then suddenly Carrie
reaches for Michael's
book. An accident
happens and tears
follow.

"*I know how you feel*"

Emotion coaching is the style that best nurtures a child's emotional development. It begins with empathy, which means valuing and sharing a child's emotional experiences. It also means helping a child learn how to handle his or her emotions in positive ways.

Everyone who cares for children can use emotion coaching. It takes a commitment to nurturing a child's emotions and a great deal of practice, and it is well worth the effort.

Here's an example of how emotion coaching works.

Michael is 5 years old and enraged because his younger sister has just torn his favorite book. As Michael stomps into the room crying, his father is faced with the difficult task of dealing with his son's raw emotional state.

Michael's father is an emotion coach, so his approach is to empathize with his son's feelings by sharing them and talking about them. He also knows that the best time to teach about emotions and to handle them is when they occur.

Their interaction might look something like this:

Michael: "I hate Carrie! She tore my book!"
(More crying)

Dad: "Come here, Michael."

Michael: "Daddy, she ruined my book!"

Dad: "I can see you're upset.
You seem angry at your sister—
and now she's crying."

Michael: "Yeah. I know. I yelled at her."

Dad: "Michael, I know you're angry. I would be too if she ripped the page in my book. Do you think it might have been an accident?"

Michael: "Yeah, maybe." (His anger starts cooling down a bit).

Dad: "I remember when my sister did something bad to me. I was so mad, I wanted to get back at her for what she did."

Michael: "Yeah. Maybe I could put her pony in the toilet."

Dad: "I don't think putting her pony in the toilet is the best way to go. We need a better solution. Can you think of something else to do?"

Michael: "Can we fix the book?"

This is only one example of emotion coaching, and every emotional event with children is different. Emotion coaching is a flexible approach, adapting to each opportunity. For the five steps of emotion coaching, read on.

Dad helped Michael to understand his emotion and Carrie's feelings too.

Robert is a little nervous. He's in a new school with many new people. He's trying to decide what to do next.

THE FIVE STEPS OF EMOTION COACHING

Emotion coaching is an approach to caring for children that values their feelings while guiding their behaviors. For many parents and caregivers, this approach isn't easy, and nobody uses emotion coaching in every situation. In fact, even those committed to emotion coaching use this approach less than half the time.

Emotion coaching takes effort and patience, and it's definitely worth it. This approach encourages healthy emotional development, so that children delight in the happy times and recover more quickly from the bad ones. Strong emotional growth also leads to better relationships, fewer behavior problems, and better school achievement. With practice, all parents and caregivers can use the five steps of emotion coaching.

1. Be aware of the child's emotions.

2. Recognize emotions are an opportunity to connect.

3. Listen with empathy.

4. Help the child name emotions.

5. Set limits and find good solutions.

Being aware of what a child is feeling is the first step towards helping him or her learn about emotions. This awareness begins with you. Those who understand their own emotions are better able to relate to children's feelings. And when you can connect with children on an emotional level, you can nurture and guide them towards healthy emotional development.

Here's the challenge: children's emotions can be hard to figure out. For example, a child may be very quiet when something is troubling him. Your job is to try to see the world through his eyes and try to uncover the emotion. Helping a child develop the language to talk about emotions is an important part of the process. But even before kids can talk about their emotions, you can learn about their feelings by listening closely to them, paying attention to their body language, and trying to view the world from their point of view.

Adults who are tuned into a child's feelings are in a much better position to offer support and understanding during times of anger, sadness, and frustration. They're also there to celebrate together the wonderful moments of joy, happiness, and laughter!

What can parents, caregivers, and teachers do?

* Recognize children's different emotions by learning what they're like when they are upset, sad, afraid, or happy.

* Try seeing the world from a child's view when he or she is struggling with an emotion.

* Listen to children during playtime for clues about what is making them anxious, scared, happy, or proud.

* When appropriate, share your emotions with them.

* Remember that children are learning about emotions by watching how you handle your feelings.

This is Roger's first
day at childcare.
Is he scared? You bet.
Who will help him
with this feeling?

As adults, we experience many emotions every day. We've also had years of practice in learning how to deal with them. But for young children, emotions are new and sometimes overwhelming. They need to learn how to handle their emotions in a healthy, effective way, and adults need to teach them. Those who take the time to listen, understand, and teach during emotional moments provide great benefits for themselves and the children.

The best time to teach about emotions is during the experience, when the feelings are real. This means sharing the moment with children when they are angry or sad, and this can happen even before the feelings grow to a high level. By talking about feelings before they grow into a crisis, issues can be handled when they are small, thus helping children learn an important problem-solving strategy.

What can parents, caregivers, and teachers do?

* Pay close attention to a child's emotions, don't dismiss or avoid them.

* See emotional moments as opportunities to draw closer to the child.

* Try to share in the feeling and encourage children to talk about their emotions, share what they are feeling.

* When appropriate, share your emotions with them.

* Let children know that their feelings are okay, and then offer guidance in sorting out those feelings.

Sarah is anxious.
Now is the time to
talk about why she
feels this way.

Listening with empathy and supporting a child's feelings—even when sad, angry, or afraid—are two of the most important steps adults can take to help children learn to deal successfully with their emotions. Helping comfort children when they are troubled lets them know their feelings are okay and that they are not alone with them. Helping children understand and cope with their emotions becomes easier and more effective when they learn to share their feelings with those who care for them.

The best way to help children understand what they are feeling is to help them put their feelings into words with simple statements. Reflecting children's feelings back to them is not only comforting, it can make them feel like someone is a friend who is on their side. It also puts the adult in a better position to help children find a solution to the problems they are facing.

What can parents, caregivers, and teachers do?

✳ Encourage children to share what they are feeling.

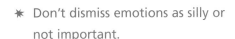

    ✳ Don't dismiss emotions as silly or not important.

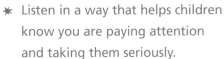

        ✳ Listen in a way that helps children know you are paying attention and taking them seriously.

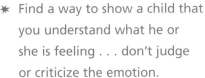

        ✳ Find a way to show a child that you understand what he or she is feeling . . . don't judge or criticize the emotion.

Kenny is upset because
Dad is leaving for work,
but a few minutes of
careful listening makes
all the difference.

Children don't always know the words they need to make sense of the emotions they feel, whether it's jealousy, hurt, fear, or worry. Research shows that when children name their feelings, they can handle them better. Naming emotions may help different brain areas communicate with each other, which can help children calm themselves. When we help children learn how to name their emotions, we give them a valuable skill that may have lifelong benefits.

Naming emotions seems like a simple approach, but sometimes it's not as easy as it sounds. First, adults need to be aware of what a child is feeling so they can help find the best words to describe those feelings. This can be tricky. Like adults, children can feel mixed emotions. To help identify what they are feeling, do a little detective work—ask a few more questions, watch the child's body language, and listen for clues in his or her tone of voice.

With some practice and a little patience, adults can help children learn the names of all the emotions they feel.

What can parents, caregivers, and teachers do?

✶ Start identifying emotions together early—even before the child can talk.

✶ Try to identify the emotions they are feeling, instead of telling children what they ought to feel.

✶ Be a good example by naming your own emotions and talking about them— children learn by watching and copying what adults do.

✶ Use the Glossary of Emotions in the back of the book as a starting point.

Is Tammy worried? Is she sad? Asking her how she feels will help her to name the emotion she is feeling.

Learning positive ways to express emotions is an important life lesson for children. The challenge for parents, caregivers, and teachers is accepting and valuing children's emotions while setting limits on inappropriate behavior.

Setting limits is the first step in any problem-solving strategy. Once adults have made it clear what children shouldn't do, the next step is to help them come up with an effective solution to their problems.

Of course, helping kids learn the best way to solve problems can take some practice. What it boils down to is:

✳ Setting goals—what do you want to do?

✳ Thinking about ideas to reach these goals—how many ideas can you think of that might help solve the problem?

✳ Helping the child pick an acceptable solution—what idea sounds like it will work best?

Children should have the freedom to experience all their emotions, and they also need to understand the difference between appropriate and inappropriate behavior. With this combination of valuing emotions while setting limits on behavior, adults can help children learn to find solutions to the challenges they will face as they grow into adults.

What can parents, caregivers, and teachers do?

✳ Discipline misbehaving children for what they do, not for how they feel.

✳ When children misbehave, use it as a time to teach by helping them understand their emotion, giving that feeling a name, and explaining why their behavior was bad.

✳ When children have a problem, start by thinking about what they want to see happen, helping them think of several ideas for doing this, and finally helping them pick a solution.

Melanie decided to read a book until it was her turn to play with the toy.

It's not always easy to be an emotion coach, and you may find that you can't always do it. However, the more you try, the better you will get at it. Caring for a child is the most important and demanding job you'll ever have, so here are some tips to help support you:

✳ Be patient

✳ Be honest with a child

✳ Avoid criticism, humiliating comments, or mocking a child

✳ Use small successes to boost a child's confidence

✳ Be aware of a child's needs, both physical and emotional

✳ Identify what the child enjoys—and what he or she doesn't enjoy

✳ Avoid agreeing or siding with the "enemy" when a child feels mistreated

✳ Empower a child by giving choices and respecting his or her wishes

And, remember, emotion coaching builds trust and leads to closer relationships between children and those who care for them . . . a benefit that is priceless.

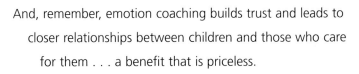

Being aware of a child's feelings is the first step to building trust. Responding with a big hug and gentle words can go a long way in soothing a child.

There's Daddy.
Where is he going?
Will he come back?
I'm kind of scared.

GLOSSARY OF EMOTIONS

Emotions are a natural part of our lives.
Understanding and identifying our own
emotions, and recognizing emotions in
children, are the first steps in becoming
an emotion coach. This glossary will help
you build your vocabulary of emotions,
so that you can become better equipped
to nurture the emotions of children.

Every child is unique, and children
experience emotions in their own ways.
By paying close attention to children's
expressions, body language, tone of voice,
and behavior, you can share the emotional
lives of the children in your care.

Glossary of Emotions

EMOTIONS TO IDENTIFY

Anger: a strong feeling of displeasure, sometimes with feelings of hostility. Children often get angry when things are taken away, or when they are prevented from doing something. They may cry, act out inappropriately, or withdraw. Their eyes will be open wide, staring straight ahead, with eyebrows bunched up together and pointing down. Their lips might be pressed together, their bodies may tense up, and their tone of voice may rise.

Emotions related to anger—a child might feel: Annoyed · Crabby · Cross · Displeased · Dissatisfied · Enraged · Envious · Exasperated · Frustrated · Fuming · Furious · Heated · Incensed · Irate · Irritated · Jealous · Livid · Mad · Offended · Outraged · Resentful

Contempt: the feeling of despising someone or having a lack of respect for something. When feeling contempt, children might sneer by pulling back one side of their mouth and rolling their eyes at someone. They might also make fun of people, call them names, or disapprove of them.

Emotions related to contempt—a child might feel: Appalled · Bitter · Despising · Disdaining · Disrespectful · Indignant · Judgmental · Offended

Disgust: active dislike for something caused by something highly distasteful. When disgusted, children will stick their tongues out, wrinkle their noses, and raise their upper lips.

Emotions related to disgust—a child might feel: Aghast · Aversion to · Dislike · Hate · Loathing · Repelled by · Repulsed by · Revulsion · Sickened

Embarrassment: the feeling of self-conscious distress, knowing that others are paying attention. Children may blush, touch themselves nervously, smile, and glance at people who are nearby. Children might get embarrassed "performing," being praised, or making obvious mistakes in front of others.

Empathy: the ability to feel what another person is feeling. Empathy can include understanding, sharing, and responding to the feelings of someone else. By the time children are two years old, they can recognize some feelings of other people and may respond to them with hugs, pats, and comforting words.

Excitement: a feeling of heightened energy and expectation that often leads to joy. Excitement can come from anticipating or experiencing something enjoyable, and it can also be a part of feeling anxious or afraid. When children are excited, they are likely to be very active and expressive.

Fear: a feeling that comes from being scared of something, or when on heightened alert, expecting that something threatening is about to happen. Children will often cry, try to get away from scary situations, and seek people or things that are safe and comforting. Their eyes are often open wide, eyebrows mostly level and curving up slightly in the middle, and their mouths will be pulled back to the sides a bit. Their tone of voice and speaking rate may rise. When afraid, stress hormone levels rise.

Emotions related to fear—a child might feel: Afraid · Anxious · Apprehensive · Concerned · Disturbed · Dread · Horrified · Nervous · Petrified · Scared · Terrified · Timid · Uncomfortable · Uneasy · Worried

Happiness: a feeling of contentment and overall well-being. Children will smile and giggle, their eyes will be bright and open, and their cheeks will be lifted up a little bit, giving their faces a joyful look.

Emotions related to happiness—a child might feel: Adoring · Affectionate · Appreciative · Connected to · Blissful · Cheerful · Contented · Delighted · Ecstatic · Elated · Euphoric · Glad · Grateful · Gratified · Jovial · Joyful · Jubilant · Loving · Pleasantly surprised · Pleased · Proud · Satisfied

Interest: a positive feeling that comes when something or someone attracts attention and curiosity. When interested, children's eyebrows will rise and might look furrowed. Their mouths might be open in a round shape as they direct their attention.

Emotions related to interest—a child might feel: Amused · Anticipation · Attentive · Awe · Eager · Engaged · Engrossed · Entertained · Excited · Fascinated · Involved · Looking forward to · Stimulated

Pride: a feeling of pleasure that comes from believing or judging that something was done well. People can feel pride in their own accomplishments or in the actions and successes of others. In children, feelings of pride begin midway through the third year. At this age children become more aware of their own goals and expectations as well as the expectations of others, and they can judge their actions based on these expectations.

Sadness: a feeling of unhappiness that comes when something is lost or a goal is not met. When sad, children's mouths will droop down at the corners, and they might stick out their lower lips. They may cry, and their eyebrows will come up together in the middle. Their posture may slump, and their tone of voice and rate of speaking may drop lower.

Emotions related to sadness—a child might feel: Blue · Dejected · Depressed · Despairing · Despondent · Disappointed · Discouraged · Disheartened · Dismayed · Down in the dumps · Glum · Grieving · Heartbroken · Heartsick · Miserable · Regretful · Sorry · Unhappy

References

Developmental Psychology. D. R. Shaffer, ed., 5th ed. Pacific Grove, Calif.: Brooks/Cole Publishing Co., 1999.

Handbook of Emotions. 2d ed. M. Lewis & Haviland-Jones, J. M. New York: The Guilford Press, 2000.

Meta-Emotion: How Families Communicate Emotionally. John M. Gottman, Katz, L. F., & Hooven, C. Mahwah, N.J.: Lawrence Erlbaum Associates, 1997.

Raising an Emotionally Intelligent Child: The Heart of Parenting. John M. Gottman & DeClaire, J. New York: Simon and Schuster, 1997.

The Relationship Cure. John M. Gottman & DeClaire, J. New York: Crown Publishers, 2001.